DuetTime® Piano

Christmas

Primer Level

One Piano, 4 Hands

This book belongs to: _____

Arranged by

Nancy and Randall Faber

Production: Jon Ophoff
Design: Terpstra Design, San Francisco
Engraving: Dovetree Productions, Inc.

FABER
PIANO ADVENTURES®
3042 Creek Drive
Ann Arbor, Michigan 48108

A NOTE TO TEACHERS

Christmas is a time for sharing with others. **DuetTime® Piano Christmas** provides your students the opportunity of sharing beautiful Christmas songs—as partners at the keyboard!

This Primer Level book is carefully arranged for the very beginning student. The primo and secondo parts are written as equals, with both parts remaining in 5-finger position. Only the simplest rhythms are used.

Melodies move from one part to another. This sharing of the melody between players offers each pianist a chance to be both soloist and accompanist, providing a special opportunity to work on dynamics and ensemble.

DuetTime® Piano Christmas, Primer Level is part of the *DuetTime® Piano* series arranged by Faber and Faber for one piano (4 hands), from primer through intermediate levels. Following are the levels of the supplementary library which lead from *PreTime®* to *BigTime®*.

PreTime® Piano	(Primer Level)
PlayTime® Piano	(Level 1)
ShowTime® Piano	(Level 2A)
ChordTime® Piano	(Level 2B)
FunTime® Piano	(Level 3A – 3B)
BigTime® Piano	(Level 4)

Each level offers books in a variety of styles, making it possible for the teacher to offer stimulating material for every student. For a complimentary detailed listing, e-mail faber@pianoadventures.com or write us at the mailing address below.

Visit **PianoAdventures.com**.

Helpful Hints:

1. The duet parts are generally notated in Middle C position for easy reading. The primo part is played one octave higher, the secondo, one octave lower.

2. Students should be encouraged to set a steady pulse for one or two measures before beginning.

3. Help the student recognize whether he or she is playing the melody or harmony; then the piano team can strive for correct balance. (Melodies are indicated by the placement of lyrics, which are not intended to be sung.)

4. A student recording of one or more of the selections would make a wonderful holiday gift. Such a recording can indicate that significant progress has been made, which is sure to please any parent.

ISBN 978-1-61677-025-9

TABLE OF CONTENTS

4

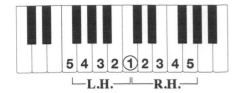

① – Thumbs share C

Good King Wenceslas

Secondo

Brightly

Traditional

(Play both hands *8va* lower)

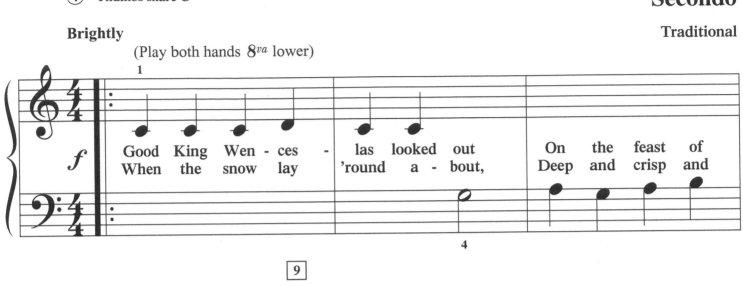

f

Good King Wen - ces - las looked out On the feast of
When the snow lay 'round a - bout, Deep and crisp and

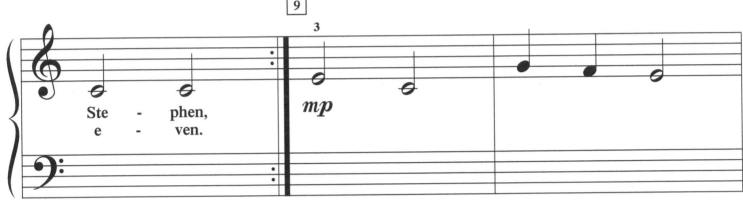

Ste - phen,
e - ven.

mp

When a poor man

mf

came in sight,

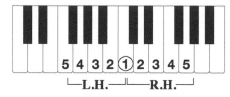

①– Thumbs share C

Good King Wenceslas

Primo

Traditional

Brightly

(Play both hands 8*va* higher)

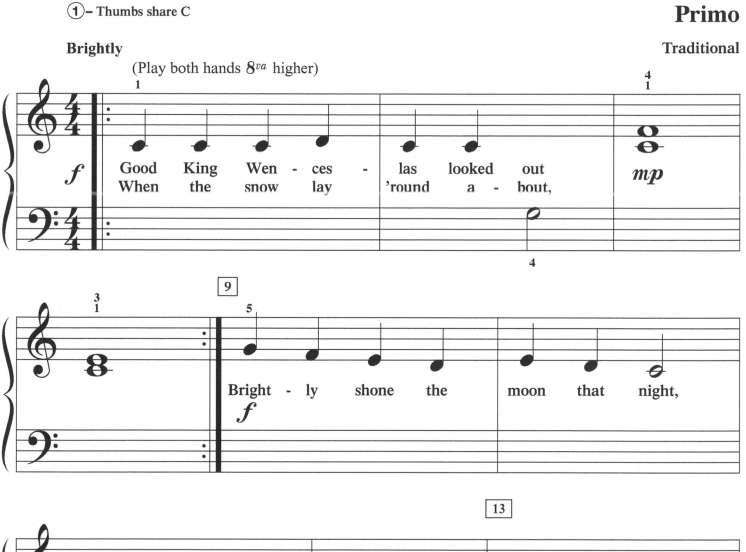

f Good King Wen - ces - las looked out
When the snow lay 'round a - bout,

mp

Bright - ly shone the moon that night,
f

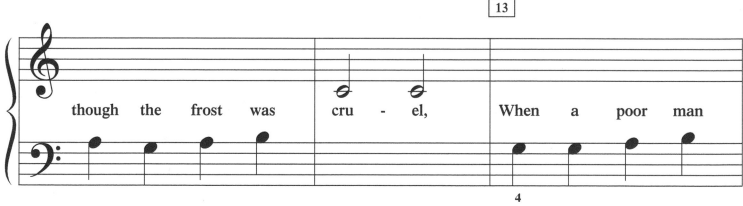

though the frost was cru - el, When a poor man

came in sight, Gath - 'ring win - ter fu - el.

Jolly Old Saint Nicholas

Secondo

Traditional

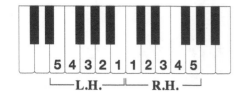

Merrily

(Play both hands 8va lower)

mf

f

Christ-mas eve is   com - ing   soon,   now you dear old   man,

mp

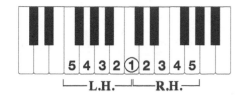

Jolly Old Saint Nicholas

Primo

Traditional

Merrily

(Play both hands 8*va* higher)

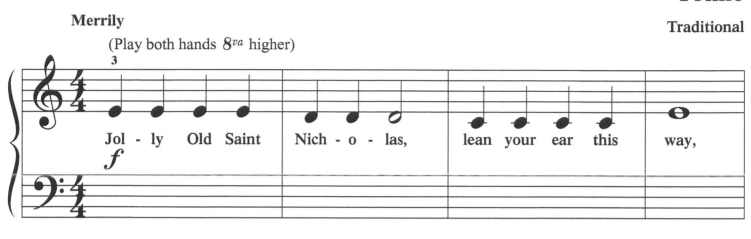

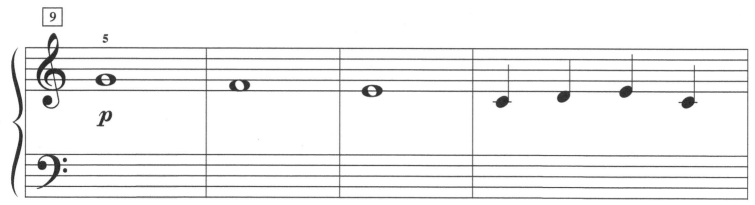

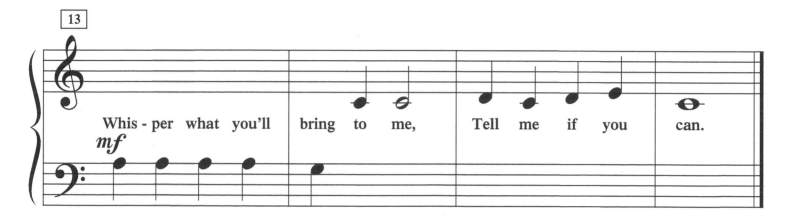

Jingle Bells

Secondo

Words and Music by
J. Pierpont

Thumbs share C

Happily

Jingle Bells

Primo

Words and Music by
J. Pierpont

Thumbs share C

Happily

(Play both hands *8va* higher)

O Come, Little Children

Secondo

Words and Music by
Christoph von Schmidt and
J. A. P. Schulz

Thumbs share C

Moving along

(Play both hands 8va lower)

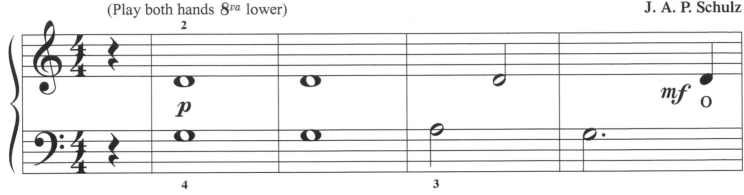

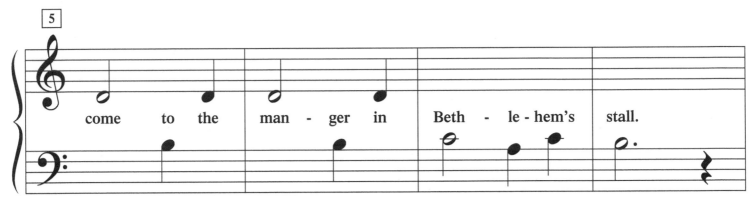

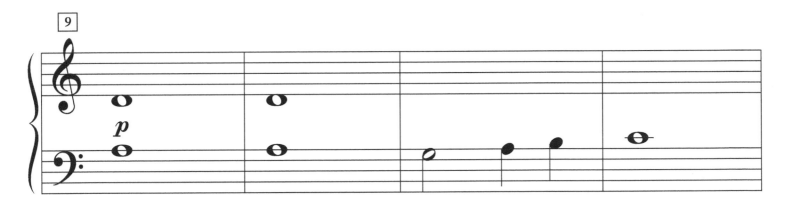

FF1025

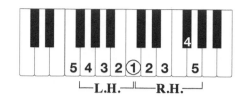

O Come, Little Children

Primo

Words and Music by
**Christoph von Schmidt and
J. A. P. Schulz**

Moving along

(Play both hands 8*va* higher)

O come, lit - tle chil - dren, from cot and from hall;

There

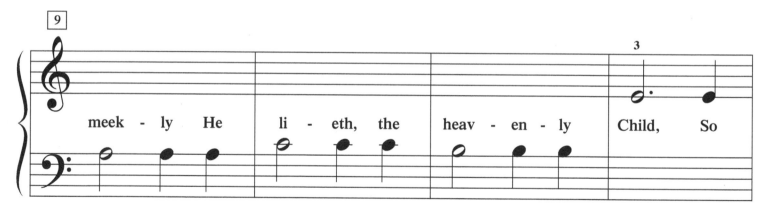

meek - ly He li - eth, the heav - en - ly Child, So

poor and so hum - ble, so meek and so mild.

FF1025

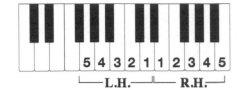

Go, Tell It on the Mountain

Secondo

Traditional

Quickly

(Play both hands *8va* lower)

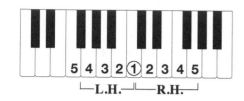

Go, Tell It on the Mountain

Primo

Traditional

Quickly

(Play both hands 8*va* higher)

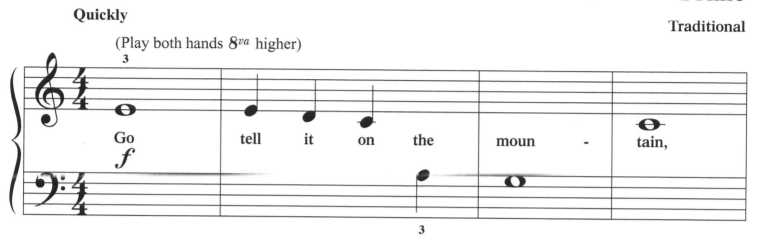

Go tell it on the moun - tain,

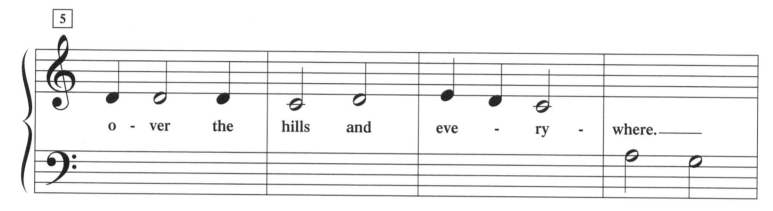

o - ver the hills and eve - ry - where.____

Go tell it on the moun - tain that

Je - sus Christ____ is born.____

14

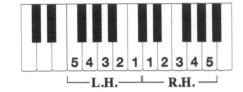

God Rest Ye Merry, Gentlemen

Secondo

Traditional

With energy

(Play both hands *8va* lower)

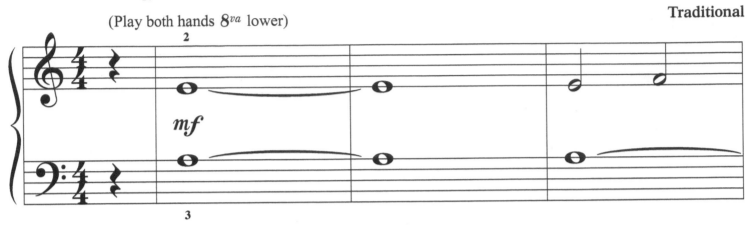

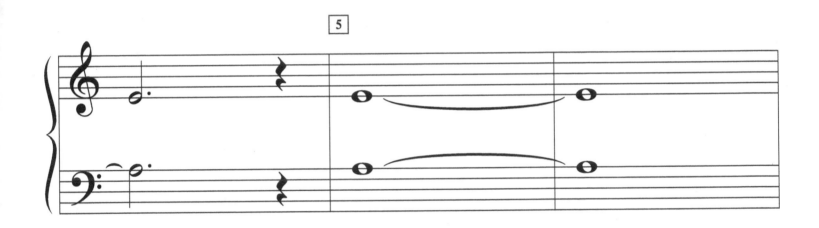

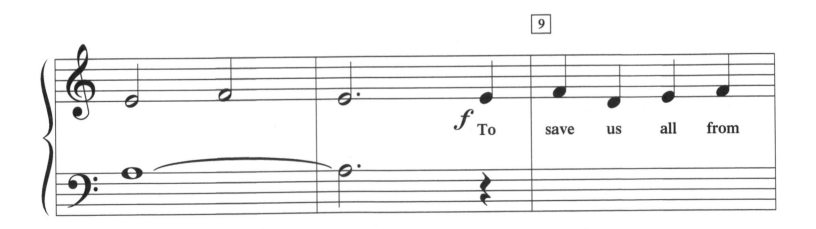

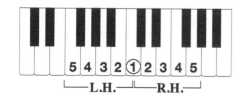

God Rest Ye Merry, Gentlemen

Primo

Traditional

With energy

(Play both hands *8va* higher)

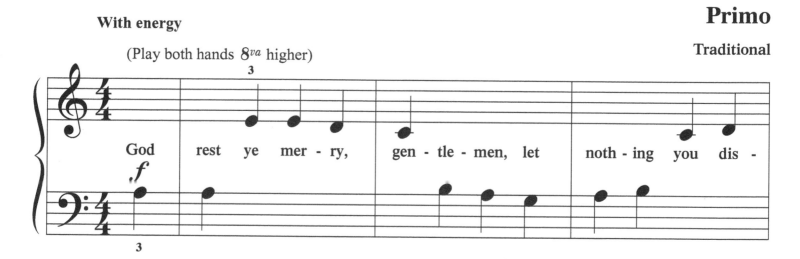

God rest ye mer - ry, gen - tle - men, let noth - ing you dis -

may. Re - mem - ber Christ our Sav - ior was

Turn page

born on Christ - mas Day, (1 - 2 - 3 - 4 -

FF1025

Secondo

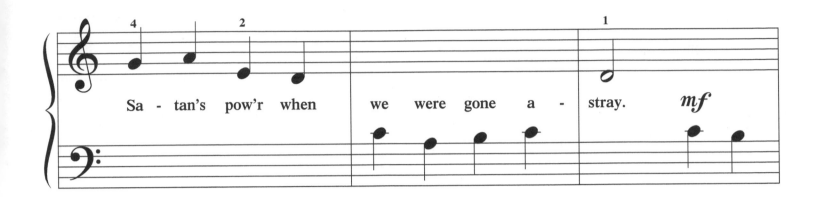

Sa - tan's pow'r when we were gone a - stray. *mf*

13

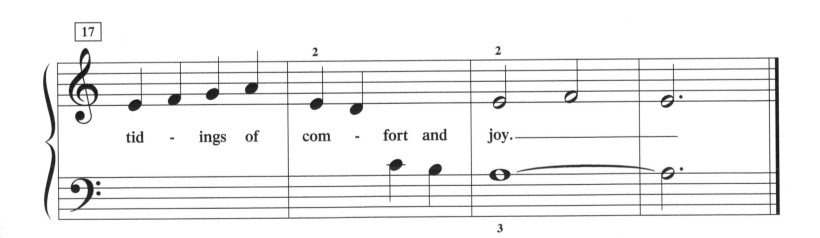

17

tid - ings of com - fort and joy.

Primo

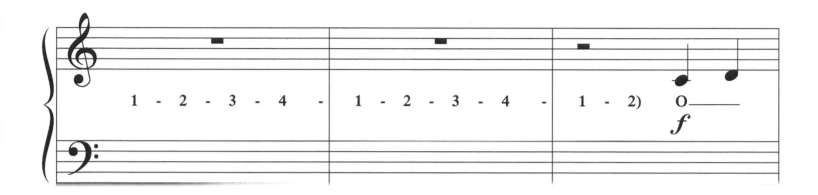

1 - 2 - 3 - 4 - | 1 - 2 - 3 - 4 - | 1 - 2) *f*

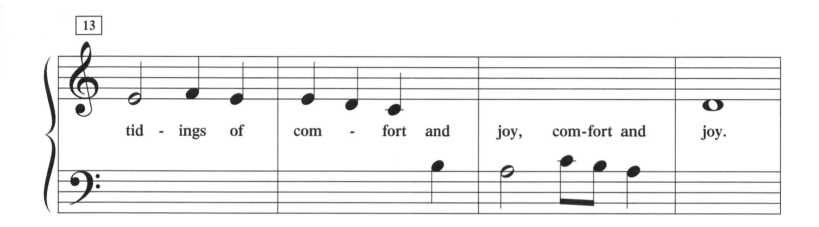

13

tid - ings of com - fort and joy, com-fort and joy.

17

4

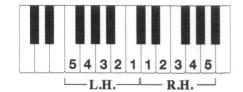

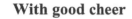

We Wish You a Merry Christmas

Secondo

With good cheer

Traditional English Carol

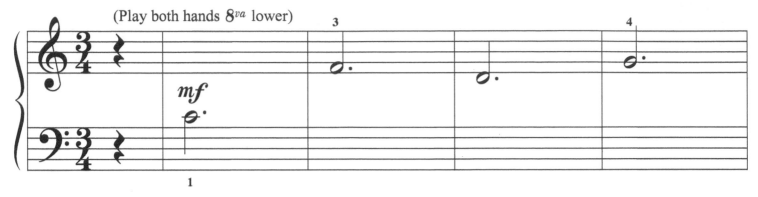

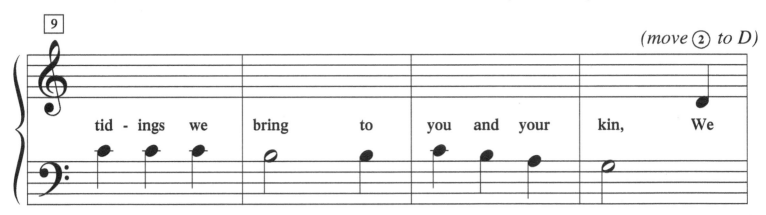

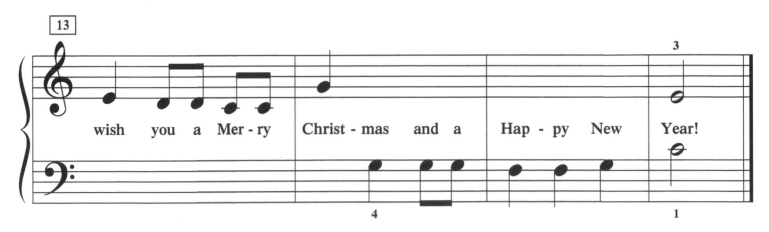

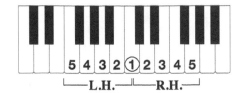

We Wish You a Merry Christmas

Primo

With good cheer

Traditional English Carol

(Play both hands *8va* higher)

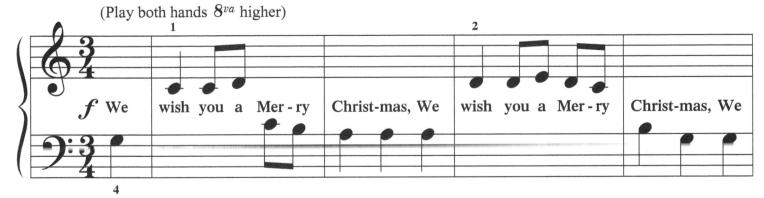

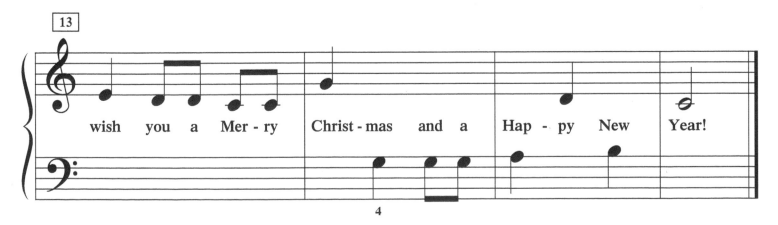

FF1025